MOMENTS
OF CLARITY

ANTHOLOGY
OF STORIES
FROM FACULTY WHO
TEACH FOR SUCCESS

Pentronics Publishing
Rio Rancho
a Teaching For Success Book

Copyright © 2014 by John H. Shrawder.

All rights reserved. No part of this publication may be reproduced, distributed, or transmitted in any form or by any means, including photocopying, recording, or other electronic or mechanical methods, without the prior written permission of the publisher, except in the case of brief quotations embodied in the critical reviews and certain other noncommercial uses permitted by the copyright law. For permission requests, write to or email the publisher at the address below:

Pentronics Publishing
721 6th St. NE
Rio Rancho, NM 87124
530-307-8549
T4S@TheGrid.net
TeachingForSuccess.com

Editor
John H. Shrawder

Contributors
Ricardo Anderson, PhD; Zenobia Bailey; Erik Bean, EdD; Dave Bequette;
Gary D. Brown, MA; Laura Roach Eyler, MA; Annie Abbott Foerster; Stacey Frazier;
Melissa Alvarez Mangual; Jana McCurdy; Stephanie A. Melick, MA; Martha Parrott, EdD;
Pamela Porter, PhD; Billy Sammons, PhD; Brian R. Shmaefsky, PhD; Ruth E. Starr, PhD;
Richard Sumpter, MPA

ISBN-13: 978-0-9740915-1-8

Ordering Information

Order directly from Amazon.com

Books may be purchased in quantity and/or special sales by contacting the editor or publisher, at 721 6th St. NE, Rio Rancho, NM 87124; e-mail: T4S@TheGrid.net

Published by Pentronics Publishing, Rio Rancho, NM
Interior Design by John H. Shrawder, Teaching For Successs, Pentronics Publishing
Cover Design by Penny A. Shrawder, Pentronics Publishing
Editing by John H. Shrawder and Penny A. Shrawder
Proofing by Stephanie A. Melick

To my remarkable spouse, artist, and publishing companion, Penny Shrawder, and to all adjunct faculty, the unsung heroes of higher education today, who overcome many personal and professional difficulties to provide high-quality, compassionate teaching for untold numbers of students

Moments of Clarity

Anthology of Stories from
Faculty Who Teach for Success

Editor
John H. Shrawder

Contributors
Ricardo Anderson, PhD
Zenobia Bailey
Erik Bean, EdD
Dave Bequette
Gary D. Brown, MA
Laura Roach Eyler, MA
Annie Abbott Foerster
Stacey Frazier
Melissa Alvarez Mangual
Jana McCurdy
Stephanie A. Melick, MA
Martha Parrott, EdD
Pamela Porter, PhD
Billy Sammons, PhD
Brian R. Shmaefsky, PhD
Ruth E. Starr, PhD
Richard Sumpter, MPA

Contents

Introduction		1
1. Teaching to Aunt Tillie	Brian R. Shmaefsky, PhD	5
2. Three Lessons of Clarity	Martha Parrott, EdD	9
3. Pilgrim of the Paradox	Richard Sumpter, MPA	17
4. On Their Own	Ruth E. Starr, PhD	23
5. A Teaching Epiphany	Gary D. Brown, MA	29
6. The Ultimate Key	Pamela Porter, PhD	31
7. Perplexity and Enlightenment	Stacey Frazier	39
8. Impossible Odds	Dave Bequette	43
9. Lifelong Candescence	Zenobia Bailey	47
10. Serendipity	Melissa Alvarez Mangual	51
11. Finding My Passion	Laura Roach Eyler, MA	55
12. On the Extra Mile	Ricardo Anderson, PhD	59
13. The Value of a Nickel	Annie Abbott Foerster	63
14. The Immediacy Principle	Erik Bean, EdD	67
15. Sheer Grit	Stephanie A. Melick, MA	73
16. Backlash	Jana McCurdy	81
17. Blazing a New Path	Billy Sammons, PhD	91
18. About the Contributors		97

Introduction: Moments of Clarity

This is an absolutely fascinating time to be alive especially if you teach in higher education. Rapid developments in technology and cognitive science rock the teaching profession from every side. Economic and political forces erode, alter, and reform the bedrock of the assumptions that support and drive higher education. Meanwhile, the subject areas of the courses faculty teach continue to bubble and foam from the constant input of new discoveries and revised theories. Keeping course material up to date is a difficult task.

Caught in the middle of these titanic forces of change are the instructional staff, especially adjunct instructors who struggle to learn and adjust the skills and attitudes required to achieve success whether teaching on campus or online.

This book is a window into the dynamic and personal world of teaching in higher education. It challenged teachers to share with the reader their moments of clarity and quantum leaps in understanding that represent the most crucial elements of effective instruction.

This anthology gives you a rare insight into how teachers, particularly adjunct instructors, experience teaching. It looks at what instructors care most about, and how each one of these authors found a path to become a better teacher.

Faculty insights into success have been the driving force behind the development of Teaching For Success (TFS). TFS is a mentor approach that marries ideas from pedagogical best practices to success strategies and principles forged by those seeking to achieve. A powerful synergy, the TFS e-Mentor Program (TeachingForSuccess.com) inspires faculty improvement and suggests ways that faculty can improve teaching for the benefit of their students. Teaching for Success means teaching for improved student achievement, retention, and completion.

These personal stories of challenge and success reveal:

- Why do some faculty teach more effectively than others?
- What do successful instructors do differently, and how do they do it?
- How do these dedicated educators think about teaching and learning?
- What has challenged them to develop their skills and deepen their commitment to successful teaching?

The seventeen instructors, who wrote about their personal moments of clarity in understanding effective teaching, are all members of the Adjunct Faculty Teaching For Success LinkedIn social network group. They responded to a post describing the idea for this volume. The anthology concept seemed the perfect vehicle for allowing a group of previously unconnected and unknown instructors to collaborate on a book about teaching success. There are many volumes written on teaching technique, but few allow teachers to describe their pivotal moment of insight that changed their teaching for the better.

The commonalities shared by this group of instructors are striking. Authors developed their teaching skills as a result of responding to one of four possible motivational experiences: a focus on student needs, inspiration from a mentor instructor, learning from a specific instructional challenge, or finding a teaching passion when encountering a subject that resonated deeply.

Most commonly, the reader will perceive the overriding concern for student success felt by these faculty authors. These instructors listen to students and resist a temptation to prejudge their motivations and capabilities.

Also, seasoned instructors in general possess the courage to experiment, change, modify, and employ new teaching strategies. They innovate and change even when adaptations lie outside their comfort zone. Their stories relate how they proceeded to try variations and then closely observed the results.

Whether you are new to teaching or have many years of experience, I trust you will resonate with the personal stories that these instructors have shared. If this anthology helps you discover your own moments of clarity as you teach for success, then the effort has been worthwhile, and this book has achieved the hoped-for value.

John H. Shrawder, Editor

1

Clarity and Simplicity

TEACHING TO AUNT TILLIE

Brian R. Shmaefsky, PhD
Lone Star College

> *The single biggest problem in communication is the illusion that it has taken place.*
> ~George Bernard Shaw

I was the first person in my immediate family to complete graduate degrees. Of the relatives who did have college degrees, there were only two that I knew of, both had studied disciplines other than science.

My close-knit family would gather frequently. At these gatherings, it became my job to explain to them the medical and scientific things I learned in college. They viewed me as the only link to making confusing technology and science jargon understandable.

There were two barriers that made the task exceedingly difficult. One was that most of my family had only a moderate comprehension of English. After all, they spoke the languages of their mother countries. Unfortunately, I was not very fluent speaking these languages. I knew enough to get me into trouble. The other barrier was that they had difficulty thinking abstractly about scientific ideas.

Science was new to them; they had little experience to encourage assimilation of theory and associated terms.

A simpler way of looking at new scientific information became imperative. I started to see knowledge in the context of: "How would I tell this to Aunt Tillie?" A wonderfully eccentric Belarusian native born in the late 1800s; she was my late fathers' aunt. Having only an informal education, Aunt Tillie was one of the relatives to whom I explained things at the simplest level. I would have to tell Aunt Tillie about science using the most accurate allegories and analogies that I could create. I still use this method to explain scientific facts to my mother and two of my brothers.

I learned to become more aware of the limitations of my knowledge through telling people about things in its simplest terms and concepts. Simplifying information becomes a challenge when it is not fully understood. Consequently, I learned to seek enough information about a topic to teach it to Aunt Tillie. The experience led me to abandon my industry and research career aspirations and seek a career in education.

The Aunt Tillie Assignment

The valuable life lesson I gained from teaching Aunt Tillie is something I instill in my biology students. I have them periodically do an assignment called, "Teaching Aunt Tillie," a creative title for this activity! Before beginning the assignment, I provide students with the backstory of Aunt Tillie. Next, they write a one-page essay about how they would present one of the current class topics to their Aunt Tillie. To be successful, a third grader should find the explanation understandable.

I grade the assignments on a Likert scale for accuracy, comprehension, originality, readability, thoroughness, and goal attainment. It is somewhat like grading an English assignment—subjectivity abounds. However, it is easy to spot carefully done labor from hastily completed work. The grades on these assignments do not have much weight towards the overall grade. I just want the students to have a tangible incentive to do the assignment.

I design most Aunt Tillie assignments as traditional essays. Some students write poetry or fairy tales. Others prefer to compose songs. One creative student translated the topic into a comic book.

At first, students have quite a few difficulties with the Aunt Tillie assignments. They find it demanding to simplify lesson concepts and devise ways to present the information. After some practice, they start enjoying it. What's more, many students incorporate it as a studying strategy. They take great pride in seeing if they can out simplify the textbooks.

Several students use the Aunt Tillie system to explain to their parents, spouses, or children what they are learning in class. They enjoy becoming the family expert on interpreting technical information found in magazines and newspapers. One student uses the technique to enhance her journalism career.

The Aunt Tillie exercise works equally well for small upper-level classes and large introductory course sections.

Various derivations can be used to manage and grade the assignments. In addition, it can be used for disciplines as disparate as biology and history—it was my moment of clarity and part of the unique way I teach for success.

References

Allen, Naomi Barbara R.. (1991). A study of metacognitive skill as influenced by expressive writing in college introductory algebra classes [doctoral thesis]. Baton Rouge, LA: Louisiana State University and Agricultural and Mechanical College.

Anson, Chris M.. (2010). The intradisciplinary influence of composition and WAC, 1867-1986. WAC Journal 21, 5-19.

Reynolds, Julie A., Thaiss, Christopher, Katkin, Wendy, and Thompson, Robert J., Jr. (2012). Writing-to-Learn in undergraduate science education: A community-based, conceptually driven approach CBE—Life Sciences Education 11: 17-25. doi:10.1187/cbe.11-08-0064 Available at http://www.lifescied.org/content/11/1/17.

2 Turning Points

Three Lessons of Clarity

Martha Parrott, EdD
Associate Professor of Mathematics
Program Chair, M.Ed. Mathematics Education
Director, NSU Mathematics Clinic
Northeastern State University

> *In learning you will teach, and in teaching you will learn.*
> *~Phil Collins*

They often sit in the back of the room but sometimes in the front. Occasionally they arrive late or leave early. Some are very diligent workers, and others do as little as they can. My students bring heartache, arrogance, insecurity, and even celebration to the classroom. This crazy mix of personalities, learning styles, cultural capital, and personal strengths and weaknesses make each day complex.

Just like many other instructors, I have gone into my classroom week after week ready to present engaging mathematics activities, organized agendas, and high expectations for student success. However, after reflecting on my teaching, I have come to realize that when I teach, my students teach me, too. I've learned many lessons, but three in particular became turning points that made me the educator I am today.

Lesson 1: Don't Give Up

Braden sat in the back of the room often slouched way down in his seat. On occasion, he came prepared, but most of the time he lacked even paper or a pencil to take notes. He would look down and away whenever I tried to make eye contact. Each day I found myself coaching, encouraging, and pushing him to be what I thought he could become.

He seemed to be a student with promise, yet he hid his potential deep down inside. Teaching him was exhausting. I felt as though I was spinning my wheels trying to reach out to a student who did not want to succeed. If ever I had a student dislike me, it was Braden. Determination kept me going even though part of me wanted to abandon the effort. At the end of each day, I felt like a wet washcloth with every ounce of water squeezed out. When the spring semester ended, I breathed a sigh of relief.

With a little rest and renewed energy, I prepared for the fall semester and enthusiastically walked into the room to greet my new students only to see Braden sitting in my class. I could feel the energy draining from within me and hoped it did not show in my face, too.

"Not another semester of coaxing and encouraging and pushing," I thought to myself. "I cannot do this again."

We made it through that first class, and as the students were leaving the room, I called Braden aside. "It is good to have different instructors who can share with students different perspectives, and if you would like me to assist you with a schedule change so you can have a different instructor this semester, I would be happy to help you transfer." What

Braden said next sparked a moment of clarity and changed me forever. He looked at me and replied, "No. I do not want a schedule change. Your class is the only one where I've ever learned anything, and I want to be here."

With that, I thanked him for his kind words and seemingly picked myself up off the floor. I pondered my own disbelief, this positive affirmation from the student whom I thought disliked me, math, and the whole learning process. The semester continued. Braden blossomed and mastered course objectives. This term produced a surprisingly different experience for me than I experienced during the previous course.

Braden's story is an early turning point in my career. While I have read how important it is to reach out to reticent students, colleagues believed that learning is the student's responsibility. They advise that after making a gesture to help, we are free to move on if the student does not respond. I disagree. Braden taught me the efficacy of reaching out to those who do not see the value in learning. I know now that I can make a difference. He taught me that persistence, energy, time, thought, planning, and high expectations are essential. To this day, when I see a "Braden" settle into my classroom, I reach down deep inside and summon the resolve to make a difference again.

Lesson 2: Connections

She was a nontraditional student, older than most. Lynn studied to make a better life for herself and her family.

However, she struggled. She seemed detached from geometry, possibly thinking the whole subject lacked relevance and purpose. She struck me as a respectful student with a gentle presence, quiet but engaged.

During instruction, her eyes never left me for even a moment, yet in spite of all her diligent work and my support, her assessment scores did not show much progress.

Lynn wanted more than anything to become an elementary school teacher. She never gave up and seemed determined to get through this required three-hour college math course. Inevitably, I began to wonder if her efforts and mine would be enough to see her through the semester.

Then, I began to talk about seeing geometry applied in a tessellation[1] art application assignment. I could see a sparkle in her eye. Intrigued, I continued with the explanation and watched her embrace the task with great enthusiasm and passion.

The day the project was due she arrived earlier than normal and quietly displayed her tessellation art assignment on her table. Her work caught my eye from across the room. The color was vivid. The images seemed to pop from the page; success. I could see her pride. We discussed her artwork; she told me of her passion for art that she had developed at a young age. Unbeknownst to me, she adored art and obviously had talent, too. It was at that very moment that she became the teacher.

Lesson learned. Effective teaching makes connections between students and their individual passions and interests. Forging contextual associations requires effort and

---

1. *Tessera* in Latin means a small stone cube. They were used to make *tessellata*, the mosaic pictures forming floors and tilings in Roman buildings. [It] ... is often used to refer to pictures or tiles, mostly in the form of animals and other life forms, that cover the surface of a plane ... without ... leaving gaps. Source: http://www.csun.edu/~lmp99402/Math_Art/Tesselations/tesselations.html.

must be intentional. The payoff is huge. Lynn's personal transformation fascinated me. Connecting the subject to a point of personal interest unlocks the door to building greater understanding. The mathematical art task turned the tide. She suddenly experienced the relevance and purpose of geometry, and another moment of clarity for me.

Her grades steadily improved. It was as though she had her own epiphany that led her to successfully completing the class. She earned each and every point meriting a B for the semester, a powerful outcome for a student who earlier failed to make acceptable progress.

To this day, I keep in my office her orange-and-black tessellation. Perhaps you have read of the importance of associations in theory books devoted to best practice, but nothing can be as vivid as seeing it impact a student right in front of your eyes. Now at the start of each new class I wonder again, What connections will make math relevant and provide a pathway to success?

Lesson 3: More than Math

"Please submit assignment number four," I announced to my class. Tamika, a high achiever, sat close to the front of the room. Sadly, she looked down toward her notebook knowing she had nothing to turn in that day. Her demeanor turned sullen. This was a drastic change from the first two weeks of the semester when she seemed happy and in control.

The severity of the mood swing told me there was more going on than a missed assignment. When class was over, Tamika stayed behind. I sensed this was my opportunity to help. I began by inquiring, "How are you today?" This simple question opened the door to a flood of despair. Listening intently, I shut the doors to the classroom, and we sat side by side for a few moments. I learned Tamika had just moved to this area. She was alone, no friends and no family and completely overwhelmed by her classes, activities, and work responsibilities.

She barely caught her breath as she tried to talk amidst the tears. I knew this was a situation beyond my abilities. Ergo, I asked Tamika if she would like to talk to someone trained to help students work through these types of challenges.

Much in need of support, peace, and tools for coping, Tamika quickly agreed. I walked with her across campus to meet with the on-site licensed professional counselor (LPC). Fortunately, he was free. I stayed by her side until the counselor was aware of the chain of events that led us there. After a few brief moments, I left; never to learn the cause of her despair.

Students as Persons

She returned to class the next week seemingly a renewed person. I noticed a new peace and resolve alive in her disposition. At the end of class, she asked to walk with me to my office. Tamika confided that she had only been an hour or so away from completely withdrawing from the university. She thanked me for caring and for seeing her as a person and not just a number on a class roster.

In the end, she continued in the course and remained enrolled in the university. Most importantly, she did not give up on her dream. While I did not accept her late work assignment per syllabus policy, Tamika did take advantage of one 12-point, extra-credit assignment available to all students. Amazingly, she completed the course with an A and went on to complete her degree. Today she teaches mathematics to her own students.

I learned from Tamika that in order to be effective in the classroom, we must sometimes go beyond the boundaries of a curriculum guide in order to meet students where they are. Creating learning partnerships enhance instructional effectiveness.

Not the Hero

I am not the hero in this story. The LPC is likely the one who helped Tamika work through her despair and ultimately suggested coping skills that led to her success that semester. Surely, it took powerful partnerships to be able to serve Tamika in her time of uncertainty.

More than ever before, students have to squeeze school into their life schedule. It is not at all uncommon for students to work multiple jobs and care for their families all while trying to take classes to achieve their academic goals. I have learned that the challenges students bring with them give teachers opportunities to respond in manifold ways enhancing the likelihood of success. Tamika's story was a turning point in my career and reminds me about what is good and right in higher education today.

Even Half as Much

Early in my career, someone once said to me that if students learn even half as much as their instructor, then the first year of teaching will be a success. As I reflect on my career, I truly hope that my students have learned as much from me as I have learned from them. To my students who have taught me through the years, thank you. You have reminded me of the importance of not giving up too quickly on those who are difficult to teach. Further, I'm sold on the benefits of devising ways to connect textbook mathematics to personal points of interest and familiarity. Most importantly, I'm clearly sold on what teachers and students can do together as partners and that these relationships in the classroom monumentally matter.

3   Developing a Framework

Pilgrim of the Paradox

Richard Sumpter, MPA
Adjunct Instructor
School of Professional and Graduate Studies, Baker University

> *There are many people who reach their conclusions about life like school boys; they cheat their master by copying the answer out of a book without having worked out the sum for themselves.*
>
> ~Soren Kierkegaard

For roughly the first 40 years of my life, I was one of those people Kierkegaard chided. What follows is my account of how that changed.

In September, 1943, at age five, I began first grade. I did not know it then, but it was the beginning of a lifelong relationship with school. For the next 70 years and counting, I was on one side of the desk or the other. For the first 35 years, I was one of Kierkegaard's schoolboys. I learned the rules and operated by them.

During the next 35 years, I learned how to break them properly. That was when my education began. Socrates, [Historians disagree on this.] said, "Education is the kindling of a flame, not the filling of a vessel." Much of my formal education was devoted to "filling my vessel." Ironically, I had to learn how to teach to learn how to learn.

On August 26, 2013, I began teaching my 208th course for Baker University School of Professional and Graduate Studies. I have taught for them as an adjunct since 1989. I have also taught for a couple of other universities during that time bringing my total number of courses taught to 275. Most studies have used the accelerated adult-learning model lasting from five to eight weeks. About a dozen programs were the traditional semester-long variety taught to 18 to 24 year olds.

Partly to Blame

I arrived to this point as a teacher through a rather circuitous route. Having completed 12 years of parochial school, in 1955, at 17 years of age, I entered St. Thomas Seminary in Denver, to begin eight years of study for the Catholic priesthood. It was a fairly intense regimen with each semester averaging about 21 hours. My major was philosophy, and I did quite poorly. Partly I blame my youth and lack of maturity, and partly I blame the fact that my philosophy textbooks were written in Latin, and I was not very good in Latin.

At the end of four years, (1955-59) I had completed about 150 semester hours of courses with a GPA of 2.4 in my major subjects. I did not earn a degree. However, I did pass the entrance exam into the School of Theology. Consequently, in September of 1959 I began my studies in theology, scripture, patristics, etc. By this time I was a somewhat better student, and four years later I completed my theology studies (another 130 semester hours). I became an ordained priest. Astonishingly, I had nearly 300 semester hours and no degree.

As an associate pastor, I taught high school religion in the parochial schools. I hated it. I completed very few studies in education during seminary training. The only teaching advice I remember was, "Don't smile until November." Teenagers intimidated and threatened me.

Public Affairs

For reasons that constitute a completely other story, I left the priesthood in 1968 after five years, and went to work for the federal government, enlisting in the War on Poverty. After a few years, I realized that promotions would require a degree, so I started night school. In 1976, I graduated from Park University (Kansas City) magna cum laude with a bachelor's degree in public administration.

Later, I found out that the federal government made available long-term training opportunities. I successfully competed for a slot in the program. By 1980, I graduated from Harvard's Kennedy School of Government with a Master of Public Administration. In the early 80s, my old professor at Park asked me to teach a couple of accelerated adult courses in their School of Public Affairs. I did. I was hooked. (In truth though, I'm not sure I enjoyed teaching as much as being a quasi-authority figure.)

In those days, we had not adopted the highly interactive teaching modes popular today. Looking back on those first courses, I approached teaching in a way that emulated my own education experiences. In other words, I taught the way I was taught. It meant a lot of lecturing. Lacking pedagogical instruction in college, my focus was on making my lectures as interesting and relevant as possible. The technology of the day was overhead transparencies; by today's standards, my teaching needed improvement.

Eureka

In retrospect, as counterintuitive as it may seem, my teaching did not become effective until my education began to gel. This maturing is still happening. After nearly 400 semester hours of rather disconnected formal schooling, my education finally began when I saw the six-hour PBS series, *Joseph Campbell and The Power of Myth with Bill Moyers*.

After reading the book that accompanied it and watching the videos repeatedly, I developed a framework for integrating my life experiences. Campbell's scholarly insights allowed me to organize my own experiences and see the interconnectedness of everything.

It is clear that a large part of education consists of recognizing relationships and finding one's place. Finally, the questions of the philosophers that I previously failed to understand began to make sense. What is truth? What is the purpose of a human being? How do we know anything? All at once, these questions became relevant and the answers understandable.

Making Sense

Armed with new insights, I was able to make sense of the theology I had studied in the seminary. I critically examined all the things I learned in my prior schooling. Some I accepted, some I rejected, and some I parked for future consideration. Campbell showed me a way to include everything. Of course, concepts vary in value, but there is a place for each one. Leaving reductionism behind, I entered a more holistic world of thought and teaching.

When I went to work for the U.S. Environmental Protection Agency in 1990 and studied ecology, I saw connections everywhere. Is nature a paradigm? No, nature is a teacher and revealer of truth in a way that is enlightening. Everything affects everything else.

I Came Alive

Once I began to formalize this worldview, I wanted to share it. I created a course on Campbell's Myth for Baker University's Master of Liberal Arts program. For nearly 10 years, I taught courses in the Business School: Business Policy Analysis, Strategic Planning, Organizational Behavior, etc. Regrettably, teaching these classes did not seem to make a great deal of difference in the lives my students.

However, once I began to teach the Myth course, my students and I came alive. This was the most enriching teaching experience I had ever had. After the term had ended, the students told me that it changed their lives. I never had a business student tell me that. I concluded it was the material that made me an effective teacher. Well, it was the material and the fact that I believed in it. In addition, I believed in an idea's power to change people and make a difference.

I went on to create more than a dozen other courses in the MLA program covering ethics, ecology, epistemology, and theodicy. I tell my students that I am a pilgrim. If they want to join me on the pilgrimage, they are welcome. I no longer see myself as an authority figure. Rather, I am the tour guide. I have not seen everything or been everywhere, but can lead students to fascinating points of interest and make the trip interesting.

4   Compassion, Buy-in and Distance

On Their Own

Ruth E. Starr, PhD

> *Power isn't control at all—power is strength,*
> *and giving that strength to others.*
> *~Beth Revis, Across the Universe*

Several audacious moments of clarity arrived when I first taught as an adjunct professor. I taught a required undergraduate-level Business Management course serving six students who needed to complete this one last class to graduate with their cohort.

I had a choice of two textbooks; one was thick with practice questions at the end of each chapter and featured an online guidebook as a supplement for students to learn more on their own. Further, the website offered the teachers notes and presentation slides for each session to follow.

The other textbook was a smaller, thinner paperback and seemed less intimidating. Therefore, I chose it as the prime resource for the course.

Presenting students with the opportunity to learn actively, I believed they would jump at the chance. I was wrong. They came to the first class expecting to be taught by a lecture format, spoon-fed the information, and then tested solely on lecture information. They sat back in their seats ready to put in four hours and go home.

During the first session, I needed to establish my "street cred" with them as a teacher of adult learners. I assigned each student a chapter from the less intimidating textbook so they could create their own presentation as part of the class participation grade. Further, if a conflict over a chapter occurred, I allowed them time to decide and barter with one another. They selected a chapter based on the strength of their personal interest in the subject matter.

Another consideration was timing. Scheduling was important because some students had other classes with assignments due at week four and six. Each chapter not selected by students was mine to cover in the class. Buy-in was critical for the group to succeed. We needed to traverse at least eight of the 15 chapters, and I did not intend to be the only person working.

I wanted the students to bond with one another and help each other out between classes. They all knew each other from other courses; I was the odd one out. I did not know them by their first names yet, but I needed to be the teacher in charge and construct the ground rules. This was my first experience at establishing distance as the instructor and acting as the boss. I even asked myself at one point, "Who's the teacher here, anyway?" I was out of my comfort zone.

Next, I planned to address the visual learners with an option to use a video from the Steven Covey's *First Things First* series. I wanted the students to see that I was not restricting lessons to the approved reference materials. In each subsequent class, I started with one of the short videos included with the book, *First Things First*. I then led a discussion about how it applied to work in the context of the chapter we were covering that day.

To their chagrin, I did not cover the chapters in order and called on the learners who came to class prepared to give their oral presentation. This practice caused some of the students to complain to the school claiming my teaching lacked proper organization. They based their assertion on their past learning experiences.

My teaching actions did not follow the norm. I subscribe to a teaching philosophy that centers on the value of students taking charge of their learning. Excellent teachers stand on the sidelines and coach. I was not going to be a know-it-all, the sage on the stage, sharing my great wisdom. I pictured us all learning from each other.

Teamwork in Action

Students in classes who self-identify as having a disability need the teacher/educator to offer options for completing their assignments without disclosing the nature of their disability in a public forum. At my school, adjunct professors must sign a privacy agreement not to disclose any personal information about their students in the open classroom.

I discovered three learning-disabled students in my class. However, only one student self-disclosed a concern. She asked for more time than usually allowed to complete the assignments. She had a hard time reading material in the time between classes. The other students in the class knew more about the problems she faced with seizures than I did. They rallied behind her and encouraged her to keep up with the reading, presentations, and written assignments. Bonding as a team, the students got the work done. I was proud of them.

I expected men and women to pick sides, but it did not work out that way in real life. It turned out that the military bonded together, helped each other by sending documents by email to each other between classes. When I noticed two of the students struggling to keep up with the work, I assigned them to the same project to accustom them to tag-teaming a presentation. They took turns presenting and adding information when the other forgot what to say. It was a pleasure to watch them grow into confident working professionals. At the end of the course, there was only one student who failed to complete the work because of an illness.

Policies

Toward the end, my school directed me to allow two more weeks for the assignments to be submitted, grade the written papers that were due, and then post the final grades. Only one student questioned his grade and wanted a consultation to discuss the differences between the actual grade and his expectations. I gave the student another chance to resubmit the paper with changes for a higher grade, but not higher than a final grade of B to be fair to the others.

One student skipped two classes but submitted the homework earlier than expected because he was on the night shift restricting available homework time to between midnight and 3 A.M.

That was an eye-opening, moment of clarity for me, realizing that the students were working two jobs and trying to keep up with family as well as write papers for school. I learned about the needs, desires, and passions that drive adults to attend classes at night and on weekends.

I understood how families make sacrifices for adult parents to complete a degree program in order to get a promotion or change career fields. I learned to respect their family time and gave them more options to meet their personal goals.

My moments of clarity helped me successfully combine a sense of professional distance in the classroom with compassion for individuals, whether disabled or not. Additionally, I saw the value of working to promote student buy-in. All of these moments helped me teach for success.

A Teaching Epiphany

Gary D. Brown, MA
Educational Diagnostician, Rapides Parish School Board
Adjunct Instructor, Bossier Parish Community College
Adjunct Instructor, Louisiana State University at Alexandria

There's nothing better when something comes
and hits you, and you think 'YES'!
~J.K. Rowling

One of my most interesting teaching moments of clarity occurred one summer. I taught an introductory special education course, a class of future teachers. During this course, I recognized that many of the students were not familiar with educational jargon that comprised my lectures.

In response, I incorporated instructional videos to clarify terms and show these teaching methods put into use. Many of my students knew of a child with an exceptionality. It was an eye opener for them to see how strategies and techniques they learned could be used to teach students with special needs.

Implementing this change was an eye-opening experience for me, too. To meet my students' needs, I moved the teaching approach beyond a traditional lecture format to include hands-on experience. Students learned practices with immediate application. They learned strategies that they would use when they became teachers.

I discovered how significantly I influenced students by sharing with them experiences that I learned as a classroom teacher. In addition, relevant learning continued when students talked with me and related their life experiences to the concepts we just discussed.

Bridge Building

Successful teaching means bridging the gap between theory and practice. Thus, it is especially gratifying to see students gaining valuable knowledge and insights and learning skills they need to enter the teaching profession.

It is one thing to lecture exclusively, but quite another to incorporate teaching methods that emphasize implementation. I realized that students learned best when they discussed practical teaching strategies with their peers. They learn deeply through a synergy of teaching application and lecture. This combined teaching approach makes instruction much more effective compared to using one modality at the expense of the other.

To learn how to teach for success, I had to search piles of information to find and master must-know teaching strategies and techniques.

A simple, but profound, personal teaching epiphany arose from completing my journey comparing effective instructional approaches that could effectively bridge the gap between theory and practice.

6

THE ULTIMATE KEY

Pamela Porter, PhD

> *[The] problem is to bridge the gap which exists between where you are now and the goal you intend to reach.*
> *~Earl Nightingale*

Students drive home the truest lessons about how to teach. Why? Many community college students are just beginning their academic lives, and they come together forming a treasure trove of diversity. That is why community colleges are an outstanding place to learn about teaching.

Instructing in this stimulating environment teaches me that the most important outcome of teaching is to bridge knowledge and performance gaps. The performance gulf is the distance between students' entrance skills and competencies required to complete their academic programs. Overcoming academic rifts entail forming strong learning partnerships. Collaborations traverse gaps by encouraging students to set their own academic goals and take responsibility for their progress.

Creating partnerships are neither easy nor entirely intuitive. Therefore, it is my practice to review each course and reflect on what worked, what did not work, and why. In the service of improving my teaching, I seek student feedback whether it is positive or negative.

Students Feedback Is Surprisingly Honest

Surprisingly, I have found students who have completed a course truly want to share with the instructor what the instructor did right and might better do next time. Accepting their feedback helps them feel part of the educational process and in control of their learning.

My first teaching assignment as an adjunct was Foundations of Learning. This study focused on learning styles, personality types, note-taking, test-taking, health, and many more life-serving skills. Serendipitously, my first section enrolled all first-generation college students. One incarcerated student came to school through a local foster group home. Exhibiting good behavior, he had earned a GED early from high school. His academic skills were very rough, but underneath the bravado he was bright and capable.

During the first week of class, I presented an overview of the course designed to alleviate answering repetitive questions about course requirements during the semester. Afterward, he asked me a very profound question, "Why had I not learned this required information in high school?" His simple question made me stop and think about how the educational system works.

The Impossible Goal

I pondered a crucial question. What is my responsibility

as an instructor? Then, my questioning student struck a philosophical nerve once again. It happened during a simple goal-setting exercise designed to teach setting short-term, intermediate, and long-term goals. This student could not identify a goal of any time length. Concentrating solely on his day-to-day existence, he had no use for setting goals. As Maslow would say, he lived at the bottom rung of the hierarchy of needs. What's more, he lacked the skills to move up the pyramid.

The Power of the Backward Timeline

How to help? I used a reverse timeline exercise to help him. This class discussion taught goal setting coupled with an understanding of Maslow's pyramid. I knew I could help him succeed.

First, I asked him to describe something that he wanted in his personal life. He thought about it. He said he wanted to see his grandmother on his 18th birthday. Aha, he had a goal. Next, we drew a timeline back from his birthday. Using the timeline, we worked together to come up with the forward action steps needed to achieve the goal. This led to the setting of an intermediate goal to pass his drug tests and a short-term goal to stay clean one day at a time.

In completing this exercise, he saw how to apply these kinds of techniques to his life. It was a profound moment. In addition, this exercise allowed the entire class to visualize course lectures and textbooks as tools for altering outcomes.

For me, it solidified the instructional wisdom of teaching from where my students are, not where I hope they would be.

I can not and should not assume an arbitrary place to start and hope that they have the background knowledge to finish the course.

YouTube and Nurturing the Seeds of Critical Thinking

Today's students have grown up in a visual age spawned by the explosion of the internet and social media. Students feel reading is not important. Learners do not see the point of searching for deeper understanding beyond the bullet points and snippets given to them in articles or tweets. Compounding the problem is that the information never stops. Given the difficulty students experience in sifting through an avalanche of information on every subject, I strive to teach more intelligently. One instructional solution is to use YouTube as an informational jumping-off point.

Seeing Is Believing

For example, I discovered a BBC video on YouTube that recreated Milgram's famous obedience experiment. Interestingly, after holding a class discussion, students stated they would never be the person who kept shocking the learner.

Then, I uploaded the YouTube video to Blackboard, dimmed the lights, and they watched the experiment unfold. I glanced around at their faces. Suddenly, the experiment had a profound effect. My students were in shock at the behavior of the people depicted in the video. As a result, the lesson took on new power and relevance. All of a sudden, students were questioning what they would do in a similar situation. The initial discussions had now become more meaningful than they were only a short time earlier.

Self-discovery, Meaning, and Purpose

Teaching general psychology is as much about self-discovery, for many students, as it is about learning fundamental concepts and principles. The key is to make the theory meaningful. Connecting it to what they see around them is crucial to their understanding and application. I explain that everything I assign and do in the classroom has a purpose. There is no busywork.

Students often ask how they will use or apply some topic. At times, students question why they are learning psychology when, for example, they are studying to become a welder. I answer them with examples that show how the skills learned in psychology apply to every field and everyone.

Testing

Next, I tackled the question of how to help students be successful with tests. I borrowed a technique from another professor. This teacher allowed students to use handwritten note cards during their tests. Evidently, when students codify information in their own words, it helps them encode and retain it. Further it relieves test anxiety.

In my classes, testing for critical thinking skills is an important outcome. I do not include questions that require simple restatements of the textbook information. They must interpret and apply what they have on their cards.

Unfortunately, some of my classes were testing higher than other sections, and I did not know why. Neither my lectures, nor the assignments had changed substantially. To find a possible answer, I reflected on my first Foundations of Learning class that achieved higher test scores. That class had contained reviews of the subject matter before each exam. I used PowerPoint to dissect typical test questions. This technique helped students understand how the questions checked their thinking skills and improved their test performance.

Also, I found it is easy for students to believe that their instructor wants to trick them or make the tests overly difficult. I needed to help my students think critically, pick the questions apart, and apply their new knowledge. The PowerPoint test analysis exercise helps students transition to the workplace. It helps them think lucidly when faced with a crisis situation.

I Just Don't Get It!

Another challenge when teaching for success is to know how to respond when a student complains that they do not get it. Perhaps a story will relate a workable approach to this common student response. Joe was nontraditional and in his 50's. He had suffered a stroke in his 20's wherein he had to relearn how to walk and eat. He rode Harley Davidson bikes and lived a tough life. His demeanor was positive and thankful that he was able to attend school at this point in his life.

The first day of class, he attentively sat up front. He recorded the lectures, took notes, asked questions, and read the textbook. He scored in the 80-90% range on every test. At the end of the semester, he thanked me and explained that he was able to understand the text because of the real-world examples I provided. In addition, because of his age, he became the focal point of many class discussions and an inspiration to the younger students. Joe taught others through the lens of his experiences.

As of now, he will be graduating with his bachelor's degree and will pursue a master's degree in counseling. He honored me by requesting that I recommend him for graduate school. Now he serves as my prime example to all my students. His efforts demonstrate that they can achieve what they want in life despite difficulties and setbacks.

Also, Joe confirmed my conviction that it is the instructor's job to relate the theory to applications students can see, feel, hear, and experience.

Partnership Clarity

In a moment of clarity, when considering all aspects of teaching, I learned that creating learning partnerships is the ultimate key to success. I see the value of transforming each and every class into a learning collaboration of responsible individuals. Here is my deal. If students read all the material, take notes, complete assignments, and study, I will help guide them to knowledge, understanding, and the ability to apply what they have learned. It is in the act of stipulating that students take responsibility for their own education that allows me to build a solid bridge to teaching success.

Bursting the Bubble

Perplexity and Enlightenment

Stacey Frazier
Language Arts Faculty
Northern Oklahoma College

> *Age is no barrier. It's a limitation you put on your mind.*
> *~Jackie Joyner-Kersee*

I realize teaching is more than standing in front of a classroom explaining a discipline to a group of very eager students. In my mind's eye, I see students as young adults willing and ready to absorb the information I have to give. However, as a teacher for a community college, this was not the case.

Here, I encountered many students from differing cultures, backgrounds, and ages. This vast population of students harbors diverse attitudes towards education. This experience burst my ideal teaching bubble, and I knew I had much to learn about instruction. I needed to learn how to teach writing to a classroom full of students who learn very differently.

One student, in particular, helped me become the teacher I am today. John walked into my remedial composition classroom on the first day of the spring semester. His presence intrigued me because, at first glance, he looked to be a little rough around the edges. I am not a judgmental person, so I just thought to myself, "I wonder what experiences he has been through in his life." Little did I fathom, this simple concern would help me vastly improve my teaching.

Perplexity Leads to Enlightenment

John was in his second semester of college. When he introduced himself to my class, he informed the class that he was 69 years old and had lived a full life prior to joining the student population. At the moment when he announced his age, the members of the class looked perplexed.

I knew the thoughts going through their heads, "Why in the world is a 69-year-old man going to college?" Honestly, I had the same notion. Experiencing that thought represented a pivotal moment of clarity in my career as a teacher.

I struggled with the doubts concerning John's motives for attending college. However, throughout the semester, John would share his experiences, and, often, I found a way to relate his experiences to the lesson of the day. This helped my students fully embrace the session as they glimpsed composition in a different light. What an amazing experience for the class!

Achieving the Dream

John joined me in my classroom for Composition I and II during the following semesters. He was a man who chose to follow his dreams of being a musician following graduation from high school. He accomplished a great deal during his musical career, but his unfulfilled dream was to earn a college degree.

Enjoyably, it fell to me to help him achieve his goal. Little did John know, he helped me achieve my aspiration of being the best teacher I could be. I thank John for helping me learn to teach for success through my students' experiences, enabling them to see writing through different eyes.

Impossible Odds

Dave Bequette
Adjunct Faculty
Butte College

Be kind, for everyone you meet is fighting a harder battle.
~Plato

In 35 years of teaching, the most challenging student I taught was a real pain at first. From the second Sylvia walked into my class with her dour expression and obvious attitude, I knew she would be a challenge. Sylvia enrolled in my computer class, an introductory-level course designed for students with little or no experience with computers. Since Sylvia was older than the norm, I expected her to have some background to draw from in the class. In spite of her age, I discovered quite a different situation, one that made me re-evaluate expectations for all my students.

Sylvia had trouble with the text from the very beginning. Not surprising, since other students in the class complained about the heavy use of long words and unclear instructions. Unlike the other students, she was very vocal and combative, my first clue that she was different. I still did not know Sylvia's story, and since I do not discuss my students with other faculty members, I did not find out important information about her for several weeks. During that time, she continued to struggle in the class. Not only did she work with the special software program available, she duplicated everything in written form. When I asked her why, she said that it helped her better learn material.

The Rest of the Story

Near the end of the course I discovered Sylvia's story, in her earlier life she earned a law degree and practiced law for many years. Despite her legal background, she did not join the computer revolution right away figuring that she had time to do that at some point in the future.

Her future became clouded by a sudden stroke at an early age, and several surgeries followed after the discovery of a brain tumor. All of her accumulated knowledge vanished in an instant, and she had to relearn even the simple tasks of life. At nearly 50, she was entering community college to reacquire what had been her life prior to the stroke.

By the end of the semester, Sylvia had become my assistant helping other students succeed in the class. Several semesters later Sylvia has nearly completed her degree. I hope the future holds great things for this remarkable person.

Holding Off Judgment

I learned from Sylvia that a teacher should not judge students by outward appearance or attitude. I assumed she had low ability, and I was put off by her attitude. It never occurred to me that she was recovering from impossible odds. Now when I see a student struggling with the text or doing poorly in my classes I hold off judgment until I know their story. I cannot imagine what it would be like to lose a career and a life of accomplishment in one moment of illness. Sylvia is an inspiration to me every day. Working with her sparked a moment of clarity about teaching.

LIFELONG CANDESCENCE

Zenobia Bailey
Assistant Adjunct Professor
University of Maryland University College

Education is the kindling of a flame, not the filling of a vessel.
~Socrates

In my moment of clarity, I saw myself both as an instructor and facilitator working in three important success areas. I teach for the sheer pleasure of kindling the learning flames for students of the University of Maryland (UMUC). During each term, my primary concern is to help define and move learners towards their course goals.

Institutional Support

Even though the UMUC Principles and Strategies of Successful Learning course is certainly a quintessential student success program, the university affords them additional help to achieve even more. It is almost impossible for UMUC students to fail if they avail themselves of these resources. In addition to being able to access their assignments, students can engage with their classmates and me, make use of an online and staffed library, and consult with an online and well-staffed writing center that will assist them with any assignment and stand ready at the students' beck and call.

I also invite guest lecturers from both the library and the writing center to my classroom for interaction and personal feedback during their workshops and conferences.

Learning Style Considerations

Let me address learning styles. I have to say that they overwhelmingly resonate with students, indeed, with anyone who spends time analyzing their own preferred mode of learning. I have noticed a definite student preference for style considerations in every single class that I've taught at UMUC and a Midwestern college.

Invariably, there is a connection between their success and their chosen learning style. Studying these learning options often helps students become better learners. Sometimes this knowledge propels them to persist when they may have otherwise quit. For me, the study of style choices becomes the core energy powering the course! Eyes light up and I-get-it messages begin to flow. Success kindled via the study of learning styles spawns the seed that sprouts into an instructor's dream course.

Learning from Students' Success

I also learn about teaching from students' definitions of success. From these, I've observed student success to be:
- About thinking and learning
- Not always about reaching a goal

- Concerned with moving forward
- Focused on showing improvement by building on a basic foundation of knowledge, brick by brick
- The development of critical thinking

In addition, students' expressions of success indicate they are building a better self-image. I saw this perception expressed as, "I am going back to school and getting my degree for me. It is not about a big job promotion; I feel that I am making myself a better person...."

Similarly, another student wrote, "I have already changed from seven weeks ago, my outlook is quite different. I already feel successful and have a long way to go. This class has helped me believe in myself; it has opened my eyes and given me hope. This class has given me a sense of accomplishment that I have not had in a long time."

Lastly, a student posited, "Student success is the never-ending pursuit of excellence through hard work and undoubted effort. In my definition, it is in the solid focus of completing the task at hand. To achieve academic success, students must have a never-give-up spirit and the resolve to strive for greatness, even in the face of adversity."

Clarity Leads to Inspiration

As each term all too quickly approaches its finish, I find it bittersweet. Still, I'm very thankful and honored to have been one who touched these lives for just a few short weeks, fanning a flame that lay within, just waiting to burst forth, finding its life-long candescence.

10 · The Value of Feedback

SERENDIPITY

Melissa Alvarez Mangual
Adjunct Faculty and Research Coordinator
Office of Institutional Effectiveness, Eastern Florida State College

The test of a good teacher is not how many questions are asked of students that they can answer readily, but how many questions will the students ask that the teacher finds hard to answer.
~A paraphrase of a popular quote by
Alice Wellington Rollins

I was a newly minted adjunct faculty when I had a surprising moment of clarity and reassurance that my methods of teaching were working. My approach to teaching is to use the class time to work with the readings and content as opposed to lecturing.

In fact, in a 75-minute class, I devote 20 to 30 minutes clarifying concepts, addressing questions, synthesizing, and drawing connections between what students develop as a result of working with the content and investigating what it means to them personally.

My Aha! Moment of Clarity

I learned a significant lesson about teaching through a defining moment of clarity. It is a lengthy story, but worth telling. It was my second semester of teaching at a small community college campus.

The first time I taught this course, 12 students enrolled. The Introduction to International Studies class was a joy to teach. It featured a diverse group of students of mixed ages, experiences, and nationalities. They all readily engaged with the content. My outside-the-norm teaching approach worked well as evidenced by the jelling of the class into a lively bunch of learners who energized each other and me.

The second time I taught the course the enrollment doubled. For the first 12 of 16 weeks, students faithfully attended class but for the most part sat quietly—with little to no interaction with one another as they waited for class to begin.

Compared to my previous class, it seemed as if I had to pull teeth to get the students to react to my questions and continue the discussion with one another during in-class activities.

Teaching the smaller class, I looked forward to each class. The students in that class would even stay after to continue the class discussions. They would visit me in my office just because they felt like it.

In contrast, instructing the larger class I had to push myself to teach energetically. In addition, I felt something was very wrong. I did not feel the students were getting it. Then, during week 14 something happened that challenged my negative evaluation about how I perceived the class was going.

Grasping the Value of Peer Feedback

Walking out of the department chairs' offices, I ran into one of the full-time, tenured professors of Humanities and Communication. We had forged a friendly relationship serving together on a hiring committee.

Greeting me, she said, "You know, we share a student."

I replied, "Really, who?"

She told me her name and I responded, "Oh, yes! How do you know we share the same student?"

My Aha! experience began as the professor related the story of her class discussion of Islam and women's veiling.

It seems several students had expressed their disgust with the practice complaining how unjust it is for women. With that point on the table, the student we shared interjected her viewpoint and formulated a question that no other student or the professor had considered. It changed everything in the debate.

A Double Standard?

She raised the issue regarding the double standard that exists and the criticism Muslims endure regarding veiling customs. The student observed that it is perfectly acceptable for a nun to go about in her habit and veil, and a priest to wear his various vestments. She added that Muslim women often decide to use head coverings as a symbol of faith and a fashion statement, too.

Continuing her discussion thread, the student added that, in many cases, the various forms of coverings serve as a leveling tool in the workplace. In addition, wearing a veil eliminates issues of sexual harassment and challenges men to take their intellectual and work contributions more seriously.

This student's contribution to my colleague's class discussion triggered a pregnant pause from her classmates, even those who had just minutes ago argued passionately against women's veiling. The professor observed that her students were now actively listening, processing, and struggling with in-depth questions concerning role complexities of the sociocultural, historical, religious, and politics involved.

Conceptual Skills Come to Light

The instructor admitted to me that she had not even considered some of the points the student expressed. Furthermore, my colleague shared with me that she had asked the student where she had learned to analyze concepts so well. The student responded, "From my Introduction to International Studies course with Mrs. Alvarez Mangual!"

It was in that moment my friend confirmed for me that despite what I had interpreted as a lack of involvement in my classroom, and a seeming disinterest in learning, this student was getting it and getting it very well, indeed! Finally, I realized that my teaching approach, even if it did not always produce immediate, observable positive results, was teaching this student to think critically. My class enabled my student to engage successfully in highly contentious discussions that she may not have otherwise been able to accomplish.

From a simple, serendipitous peer conversation, I had learned the value of receiving good feedback on the effectiveness of my teaching from others rather than depending on unquestioned assumptions gleaned solely from my personal observations.

Finding My Passion

Laura Roach Eyler, MA
Associate Faculty
Cascadia Community College
Renton Technical College

> *You can never really live anyone else's life....*
> *The influence you exert is through your own life,*
> *and what you've become yourself.*
> ~*Eleanor Roosevelt*

I do not know if motivation can be separated from desire or when desire turns into motivation. All I know is that for as long as I can remember, my mother told me I'd make an excellent teacher. Of course, who listens to their mother? It took me a while to agree with her assessment. Here's my story.

Since I was a good reader, teachers asked me to sit with other children in class and help them read. Thus encouraged, I would help them sound out words and project emotion. In the summertime, my mother took me to students' homes to help poor readers learn to read better.

Also, my dad encouraged me to play with children who did not speak English. He set up a play date for me with a Mexican family who had moved into the school district. None of the children spoke English, and I certainly did not speak Spanish, but we played together. Then, one of my church members hosted some children known as the Vietnamese Boat People. I naturally wanted to help them learn English. Surprisingly, I did. As time went on, our ability to communicate with each other improved dramatically.

I Will Never Teach!

It was a high school geometry class, and we had a brand new teacher. Not only was she new, she was not any taller than me (and I am short). She had an acne problem, buck teeth, and a Dorothy Hamill haircut. She never stood a chance. The boys cat-called, asked confusing questions, and they argued making the class a torturous experience. One day, they made her cry. I felt awful for her. I swore I would never teach! Time passed. I graduated high school, then earned a BA in French, and finally, I became a proofreader.

Enlisting in a Cause

Motivation to teach came to me during my proofreading years. I could not understand how Americans could write so poorly after years of school. Had not they listened in class? And, what about the millions of nonnative English speakers? How did they learn English? A coworker overheard me pondering these questions. She suggested I look into a program at Southern Illinois University at Carbondale (SIUC). The school had a program called Teachers of English as a Second or Other Language (TESOL). Wow! Did that mean I could travel internationally and teach at the same time? I think it did.

The Right Program for Me

With the help of Dr. Redden, head of the Linguistics Department, SIUC, I signed up for the Applied Linguistics program so I would be prepared to teach phonetics, linguistics, and ESL. While studying Applied Linguistics with a TESOL minor, I applied to work in the Center for English there. My first day in class was enlightening, and finally, I knew I had found my calling.

Now I understood the joy radiating from one of my teachers when he said he loved the sound of pencils writing. No compliment is better than one given to me by a student who reports he can hear in my voice the encouragement he needs to master English. Motivation continues when a student thanks me for being his/her teacher. There is a sense of bliss in doing what I love to do. Mother was right after all. I clearly had found my passion.

12   Staying Flexible

On the Extra Mile

Ricardo Anderson, PhD
Adjunct Instructor
International Business School of Scandinavia

An effort made for the happiness of others lifts us above ourselves.
                               ~Lydia M. Child

My first teaching assignment as an adjunct instructor at Concordia University taught me the value of staying flexible and responding to students' needs.

As a beginning instructor, I did not know what to expect from a group of adults who had families, worked full-time, and pursued leadership positions at their current jobs.

The format of the course required each student to complete pre-assignment readings with written responses to discuss their views about various scenarios in leadership and management. This class format immediately sparked conversation about these workplace issues. Listening to adult learners engage in discussions covering these weighty topics constituted an amazing experience for me.

During this four-week program in Organizational Management, the students' written assignments required APA format, including their final paper and critically written responses to the course readings. At that time, the university required research papers written in the MLA format, but it now began a transition to APA criterion.

Change Breeds Anxiety

The students were understandably nervous. They were not familiar with APA standards. For many of the students, this was their first class that required APA format and documenting research using information technology.

The second and third class sessions met in the computer lab where I explained APA format, citations, and references. I added examples to clarify standards.

I allowed students to form groups to share their responses to the APA paper, their first writing assignment. The defining moments in this process were:

- Assisting students to set up a research structure
- Beginning the research
- Initiating writing about their influential leader
- Creating options

Next, I visited each student in the computer lab and asked him or her, "What would be the most effective way for you to present your paper inquiry to us?"

Some students expressed a preference for PowerPoint, others liked videos, and a few used the interactive SMART Board.

The Extraordinary Final Class

The level of knowledge growth and high-learner enthusiasm that permeated the room amazed me. By the end of this series of classes, my students were confident. They were off to a fabulous start. Some students had even progressed rapidly to the halfway point with their assignment.

Most importantly, the final class was extraordinary. I watched the students confidently and skillfully present their research. My dean commented that my students told him I was a great instructor, and they appreciated the time and extra effort I put in to the course. The Dean also explained how these adult learners had palpably felt the sincerity of my teaching commitment. My flexible approach enabled them to experience success and not feel intimidated even though they did not, at first, understand how to produce an APA-formatted paper.

The Dean appreciated the way I was able to integrate the course content and meet the distinctive needs of these students. The outcome was a success for everyone involved. All my students flourished, and everyone passed the program. What's more, I taught for success, attaining a 100 percent student-retention rate.

13

THE VALUE OF A NICKEL

Annie Abbott Foerster
Adjunct Faculty
New Hope Christian College

*Imagination does not become great until human beings,
given the courage and the strength, use it to create.*
~Maria Montessori

I went to a public elementary school in a small California coastal town. The year before President Kennedy's assassination, I attended 5th grade. My teacher was Mr. Robert Nelson, a middle-aged, single guy, who taught with enthusiasm and kindness. As was the custom, Mr. Nelson wore a suit to work every day, complete with a long-sleeved white shirt and tie. He and the band teacher were the only male teachers I had to that point. We thought he was very cool.

The Challenge
Mr. Nelson wanted to take us on a field trip to the San Francisco Zoo. This was a big deal. The destination lay more than 100 miles distant. The school district did not have the money to pay for such an adventure, but they said if we raised money for the driver and the bus, we could go.

Mr. Nelson told us that if we wanted to go, we had to figure out how to raise money. First lesson in brainstorming, first lesson in finance, and a big lesson in responsibility!

The Plan

He split us into groups; each group presented their idea in front of the class. The class chose a bake sale; everyone contributed homemade cookies and cupcakes, and we sold them at lunchtime in the cafeteria. The class sold everything, but we were still short of funds.

Then Mr. Nelson asked us what we thought of this plan. "My mom makes the best peanut brittle in the whole world, and she said she would share her special recipe if we wanted to make it to sell. Would you like to do that?" Our excitement grew exponentially. "OK, then let's figure this out, and list what we need to know."

We started considering key questions such as how much:
- Money is needed for the trip?
- Candy would we need to make?
- Should the candy sell for?
- Will the ingredients cost?

He followed by inquiring how we would promote the product and what the advertising posters would look like. He asked us to write a list of supplies we would need. Finally, we drew plans, goals, and schedules; clever, Mr. Nelson!

Action Steps

For readers who are not candy makers, please note that the first step involves heating granulated sugar until it becomes boiling sugar syrup (easily capable of spattering and inflicting burns). The next step in making peanut brittle involves stirring baking soda into the boiling syrup so that it climbs joyfully up to the top of the pan becoming a formidable, foamy boiling syrup.

Lastly, add peanuts, and continue to cook and stir constantly. Finally, pour the boiling candy onto a greased cookie sheet. After it cools, crack it with a hammer! Imagine letting 5th graders loose with this recipe for disaster in the classroom today! I learned that great teachers often step out beyond convention to make a point, albeit keeping safety in mind.

The Pay Off

We sold the peanut brittle in one day. We sold it to parents, neighbors, and relatives, selling each stapled waxpaper bagful for a nickel. We learned the sweet satisfaction of participative success.

In the end, I did not go on the trip, but I never forgot the lesson. None of this came out of a textbook. Dear Mr. Nelson is somewhere in my thoughts each semester as I plan my undergraduate classes; the effects of this one project have lasted a lifetime. I learned that the best lessons are participatory, born of creating imagination and motivation in learners; planning in teams for the greater good extends this thought and creates communities.

Dreaming Big

I learned that the power to dream big inspires innovative leadership, even for 5th graders. I understood that relational teachers take off their coats and roll up their shirtsleeves, actively participating with their students as they learn. This was unheard of in Mr. Nelson's time.

I learned that a kind and patient guide on the side combined with experiential learning forge a powerful lever to boost learning. This approach ties all sorts of unexpected things together to create something that is bigger than the sum of the parts. I'm sure that each one from that class still carries with them something from that experience.

There were so many ways in which this lesson was generous, gracious, meaningful, and impressionable. Many years later, it suddenly dawned on me that Mr. Nelson had donated all of the ingredients for the peanut brittle, and built the heart of a new teacher.

The Immediacy Principle

Erik Bean, EdD
SocialMediaLessonPlans.com

> *Example is not the main thing in influencing others.*
> *It is the only thing.*
> ~Albert Schweitzer

When I teach, I engage every student. It is a misconception that levels of student attentiveness vary, lower for an open-enrollment class or higher for a course in a student's major. Even some of the sharpest, most focused students, struggle with attentiveness issues. My moment of clarity story shares effective ways I found to allay attentiveness issues and teach for success.

Undoubtedly, in order for a teacher to be successful, in a traditional or online classroom, the students must be attentive. However, on one hand, the student must be mature enough to be passionate or, at minimum, inquisitive to maintain focus. On the other, the instructor must be engaging, thought-provoking, contemporary, and on top of the issues in his or her discipline. Finally, a sense of immediacy is equally important.

Immediacy and Success

Similarly to delivering any memorable and convincing speech, the teacher must establish goodwill early in the course. This too occurs by being engaging, thought-provoking, and excited by the subject. Students size up a faculty member in the very early moments of any class. Consequently, on the first day, it is lights, camera, action! To be successful, one must lead by example. The definition of immediacy is, "the immediate presence of an object of knowledge to the mind, without any distortions, inferences, or interpretations, and without involvement of any intermediate agencies" (Dictionary.com, 2013, para 7).

In the early 1970s, Mehrabian, a scholar at the University of California, popularized the immediacy principle. Regarding the immediacy principle, Mehrabian (2007) said, "The association of immediacy with liking, preference, and generally good feelings, on the one hand, and the association with nonimmediacy with dislike, discomfort, and other unpleasant feelings [on the other] lead to numerous applications" (p. 109).

Body language and eye contact convey a sense of immediacy particularly due to their nonverbal communication cues. Another example of immediacy includes referring to students by name in discussions and other class activities.

Ownership

No matter the topic, I begin each new course by offering motivation in the form of philosophies that put the ownership of success squarely on the student. I find this works well for open-enrollment or competitive-entry students. I offer my advice not talking down, but rather uplifting students.

The Gazelle

For example, "Every morning in Africa, a gazelle wakes up, it knows it must outrun the fastest lion, or it will be killed. Every morning in Africa, a lion wakes up. It knows it must run faster than the slowest gazelle, or it will starve. It does not matter whether you are the lion or a gazelle—when the sun comes up, you had better be running." [According to QuoteInvesitgator.com this quote is attributed to securities analyst, Dan Montano, writing in *The Economist* in 1985.] For an online class, I post this quote in the welcome message. In class, I read it with conviction in the best story-telling sense.

I also show a motivational video such as the one at www.212movie.com. I am not affiliated with this business, but the video certainly makes quite a bit of sense and students can easily identify with its simple paradigm.

Smartphone Use

Every generation brings new challenges. Smartphones are pervasive in the classroom. Many students use their phones to take notes and are serious in this endeavor. While these devices can serve educational purposes, some students use them unwisely.

One method of combating trivial smartphone use is to employ it as an active teaching device. For example, consider the use of social networks to teach writing or public speaking, or specialized apps for humanities and science investigations.

Student Self-participation Ratings

Regardless of the level of smartphone use allowed, consider having students rate their own level of engagement after each course. Self-ratings occur by handing out a simple participation rubric. For example, this rating form could include categories such as superior contributor, satisfactory contributor, low–level contributor, and noncontributor. This method puts the burden of accuracy on the student. It promotes the ethic of accuracy and fairness.

Timmy, Well, You Know…

I have found improving attentiveness using immediacy and student-participation ratings produces overall positive results in my on-site and online classrooms.

Employing these techniques equate to the 1950s *Lassie* television program's moral lesson exemplified by the phrase, "You see, Timmy…." By emulating Timmy's mentors, faculty can strengthen student rapport and improve attention levels by fashioning better lectures, employing smart technology, guiding interactive discussions, and incorporating social media.

A Special Relationship

Finally, I remain mindful that students are customers. I stay humbled by the special relationship I enjoy as a teacher with them. The knowledge I gain from student feedback and their perception of the course is an educational gift I do not take for granted.

References

Mehrabian, A. (1971). *Silent Messages*. Belmont, CA: Wadsworth.

Mehrabian, A. (2007). Nonverbal Communications. New Brunswick, N.J: Aldine Transaction.

15

Finding Meaning

SHEER GRIT

Stephanie A. Melick, MA
Adjunct Instructor
Centenary College and Caldwell University

Stories are the single most powerful tool in a leader's toolkit.
~Howard Gardner

As an adjunct instructor for an accelerated continuing adult degree program, I often wonder who is learning more: the students or me. Every day, the media provide stories of amazing determination, designed to inspire and motivate me, and they certainly do.

However, the stories of an entire group of learners remain unpublicized. These are adults who have decided it is time to become college students; some for the very first time.

I teach their first course Academic Foundations (AFC), with the major objective to acclimatize the adult student to college and academia.

It is through this class that I am privileged to hear the backstories that brought about their return to school. Each student offers a unique saga of determination and inspiration.

Unsung Heroes

It is the story of a student, who, after an unsuccessful first college experience and making choices resulting in multiple run-ins with the legal system, now appreciates the learning experience. He is proud to say he is a 37-year-old sophomore.

It is the narrative of a returnee to school after 20 years as a single parent. She is successfully raising two children, juggling home, work, and academics, focused by a life-perspective born out of struggle and deprivation. Once disenfranchised, she now believes she can make a difference.

Denial No More

It is the tale of an initial denial to higher education due to her immigration status, even though she graduated 7th in her high school class. Now with a green card she embraces the opportunity to obtain her college degree. Having known bigotry and bias, she now seeks to become a role model for those still denied access to education.

It is the saga of working three jobs to support a family and thereby setting a heroic example for his five children. He is now achieving excellence in the classroom by employing his intellect and leadership skills. This man fully understands the true meaning of challenge.

It is the history of a student who has experienced years of domestic violence, finally accepting that she has worth, intelligence, and a voice. Now she seeks to prove not only to those who once demoralized and degraded her, but mostly to herself that she can succeed.

It is the anecdote of a man who witnessed corruption on the job and reported it. He now wants to make a difference in how companies do business by learning how to implement values and integrity into the day-to-day operation and organization of corporate America.

Finally, it is the report of a veteran, who, after tours in Iraq and Afghanistan, is a single parent trying to raise a two-year-old while dealing with traumatic stress. She is now proving herself in the classroom, just as she did on the battlefield.

How Backstories Inform Instruction

Every one of these students has the desire and motivation to succeed, yet they need support and guidance to do so. Encouragement comes from family and friends and the learning institution and their instructors, they all have an obligation to support these students.

I believe that my role as an AFC instructor is to provide the adult students with academic benchmarks and skill-sets needed to make the grade and to teach a set of values applicable in every aspect of life.

Students learn with the help of clearly stated parameters and transparent school policies set forth in syllabi. Also, my students need me to be accessible to them. My assistance must be available in a nonjudgmental and trustworthy form. In addition, I provide meaningfully relevant lessons and topics for discussion.

The adult students also need my empathy. It enables me to understand them without condescension. Finally, institutions of higher learning and I need to provide the adult students with the guidance to navigate through an all-important, yet exasperating, barrier, dealing with organizational minutiae. This last factor has caused many students to throw in the towel on their first attempt in college. I believe that if I can implement a people-oriented humanistic approach, students will succeed in obtaining their dreams.

Core Values and the Classroom

How then do these core values translate into the classroom lesson? Well, many of my students still are not sure what role they will play in the workforce. They struggle to find work in an economy that fills menial positions with degreed individuals.

Therefore, the former guidance counselor in me uses a variety of self-assessments, inventories, and surveys selected to help students identify strength and weaknesses, interests, and motivators. The results enable each student to create a personality and skill-set profile, a picture of whom they are both in and out of the classroom. One of my students dubbed these tools the "Cosmo quiz of the week," but at the end of the course confessed that if he had known himself this well 20 years ago he probably would have made it through his first attempt at college.

Another task asks students to compare and contrast group roles against Maslow's Hierarchy of Needs. This lesson considers worker reticence to demonstrate leadership qualities in a business setting. Are they acting from fear of rejection or the possibility of losing their job? This leads to a discussion regarding how one's metacognitive awareness can determine work satisfaction. In fact, after every assessment, we examine the results in terms of the student's current personal and professional life issues.

The assessment interweaves benchmark skills such as comprehension, critical thinking, and writing that are necessary to continue in an associate's or bachelor's degree. All this leads to the writing of a career analysis research paper that helps the student learn about his or her dream job. Also, it refreshes skills in or introduces the student to information literacy, database research, and a formal research paper.

These academic skills sometimes baffle and frustrate my students. The tough question that inevitably stymies them is "Where do you see yourself in five or ten years?" This is not surprising, considering the average age of my continuing education students is 35-40 years old.

Where Do You See Yourself?

Two encouraging stories come to mind. The first is about one of my students who stated that her dream was to become a CEO of a hospital. Currently working as an office manager in a doctor's office, she believed this was a natural progression. She was able to identify the business courses required to achieve a BA and eventually an MBA. She found academic and peer-review articles on the qualifications and responsibilities of a hospital CEO in the library databases. She even found two people whom she could interview and/or shadow. After setting up her paper, addressing all the bullets of the assignment, she interviewed a CEO. Then she called me in a panic.

After doing all the research and interviews, even shadowing the CEO one afternoon, she realized that she did not have the personality traits for the job. How did she know this? She compared the results of all the inventories and surveys she had completed during AFC and realized that her results were antithetical to the characteristics needed to run a hospital.

For example, there is quite a bit of administrative paperwork required, and that was not even a blip on her career-interest survey results. She also realized that she needed strong leadership skills and her results from the teamwork inventory indicated that she was much stronger in compromising than average. The only assessment that would have supported this future career choice was the results from her learning-style survey, that indicated she is a physical reflective learner; learning styles that would be needed when one is in charge of an entire hospital.

Now What?

Her panic stemmed from a due date of less than three days hence! What should she do now?

My advice was to finish the paper. Explain what she discovered and how this assignment benefited her by saving her years of course work. What a wonderful example of academic learning informing a major life decision.

Further, as an endnote, she changed her major after realizing that she was more interested in the qualitative rather than quantitative aspects of a business. She is now earning a bachelor's in sociology, concentration in organizational studies, rather than a bachelor's in business administration!

The second story is about a student who was currently working in a high-paying, high-stress sales job. The 10-hour days were wearing. With a growing family, he simply could not walk away from the steady paycheck. Used to hard work and long days as a former Marine, he became uninspired and bored. He could not answer the question, Where do you want to be in five or ten years? He just knew it was not in his current job.

The career-interest survey indicated he would make a good crossing-guard! Seriously, that was his top career match. We all had a good laugh at that; unfortunately, the results were valid. His learning style was a physical, social learner. His teamwork skills were strong in leadership and evaluation. He was the first to acknowledge the uncanny accuracy of the organization-skills assessment. He concurred that he lacked organizational and time-management skills. Crossing guard was looking more and more viable!

In the end, it was his love of food that won out. After interviewing a couple of friends who owned restaurants, he concurred that indeed his interest would be held by the day-to-day minutiae of running a restaurant. The café environment would keep him moving while allowing him to kibitz with people. He was also wise enough to understand that he would need a partner who possesses the organizational skills he lacks. No worries. He would be the host, the face of the restaurant and his partner could be the brains. He knows just the right person for the job....

Clarity

Stories like these are the reason I teach. My role as the instructor is to encourage and enable efficacy in the academic world. I also urge my students to embrace the learning—not the grade. In every course, I strive to embolden students by focusing on their strengths and to encourage them to ask for help, a difficult action for adult learners. Therefore, as an adjunct teaching in an accelerated adult program, I embrace the core values that foster endurance and resiliency. Essentially, I develop and earn my students' trust, manage learning, and cheerlead. However, students' desires and beliefs make the difference.

Out of sheer determination, these adult students walk into classrooms every day anxious at the impending challenges, yet eager to absorb and share the learning. They may not be the current sound bite who gets their 15 minutes of fame, but they are superstars in the eyes of their families, friends, and especially me. As a wise man once suggested to me, anything I can do to nurture and strengthen this determination will pay unbeatable dividends. It helps students achieve their dreams. These were my moments of clarity that influenced how I teach for success.

16

Convergent and Divergent Backlash

Jana McCurdy
Department of Social and Human Relations
College of Western Idaho

The path of least resistance and least trouble is a mental rut already made. It requires troublesome work to undertake the alternation of old beliefs

~John Dewey

Traditionally, college instructors possess refined convergent thinking skills comprised of diligent planning, orderly lesson planning, lecturing on content that corresponds well to tests and assignments, and being organized and predictable.

However, divergent thinking yields greater creativity. This teaching modality is important because it encourages instructors to try new methods and respond spontaneously to the classroom environment. Therefore, effective instruction balances both convergent and divergent approaches. In addition to teaching knowledge, college instructors teach important thinking skills such as critical analysis. Thinking-skill improvement is necessary since all people, not just students, resist changes in established thinking patterns and strategies.

This is an account of how a moment of clarity in my instructional thinking benefited my psychology students. The change was in response to their need of a better way to understand underlying concepts and think more systematically.

Going Beyond Personal Experience

Psychology is fun to teach. Most of the students eagerly study human behavior and those reluctant ones usually become quick converts. Teaching a relevant and practical class evokes many advantages. Even so, during the semester, the students and I occasionally arrive at an impasse because of their established biases that become highly resistant to modification. Convincing students of the existence of dynamic forces beyond their own experiences and impressions is often difficult (Savion, 2009).

Talented teachers continue to experiment with various methods and gradually improve their techniques from one course iteration to the next. The examples presented here are challenging and frustrating topics to address in the classroom. I found that statistical concepts become the key to helping students visualize complex social phenomena. Graphic information is effective in reducing cognitive ambiguity and balancing conflicts.

When Students Reject Facts, Now What?

Undergraduate psychology classes often investigate the relationship between playing violent video games and aggressive behavior. Controlled experiments (Anderson and Bushman, 2001) establish a direct causal relationship. However, the complex research comes not without considerable debate regarding operational definitions and validity. Strikingly, asking students to accept these findings kindles derision. The problem stems from the correlational, not causal relationship, described by much of the published research related to video games and violence.

A Backlash Developed

At first, I presented via lecture the relationship between violent video games and aggression. Stony faces and disbelief met my efforts. Then, I tried improving the lectures with additional research studies, quotes, and video clips. Unfortunately, the disbelief continued. In subsequent classes, I introduced research papers, debates, and worksheets. I continued to rely on convergent thinking—I had a logical plan and information to share and attempted to perfect my lesson plan to present this information more persuasively. Rather than becoming more persuasive, a backlash ballooned—students became more and more skeptical and resistant.

Preconceived Ideas Are Tenacious

They held tightly to their preconceived ideas in the face of contradictory information. Each and every time we discussed video game violence, a significant percentage of the students refused to consider the possibility that violent video games had any effect whatsoever on behavior. Why should they? They had their own history and experience. They played violent video games with their family and friends and were peaceful people. Students would agree that some people have risk factors that might make them susceptible to increased aggression after extensive exposure to violent video games, but surely that was the result of their risk factors and not gaming.

Trends and Outliers

One semester, in frustration, I did not address the topic. Other semesters I brushed over the topic in a cursory manner accepting that I could not substantially change prior convictions. In hindsight, resistance is not a valid reason to excise a topic from the course. Changing long-held beliefs may occur in small increments like water eroding a large boulder.

The process of divergent thinking started with a simple insight into trends and outliers. With the aid of a textbook showing a scatter diagram, I led a discussion on variation. This was a new approach that had not been tried. (See Figure 1.)

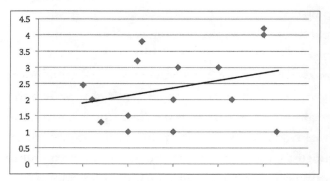

Figure 1: Hypothetical scatterplot showing a linear line of best fit (correlation value r = .3).

Getting the Picture

When it was time to discuss correlations I drew assorted scatterplots and lines of best fit on the whiteboard. We talked about r values and positive and negative correlations. I showed them r values of .9, .7, .3, and 0. Visually they look very different. R values of .3 are significant but still have a tremendous amount of variation. This is the level of correlation that is recurrent in social and behavioral sciences because humans are complex creatures operating under different interacting variables.

I circled two of the outlier data points and showed them that one person could play a lot of video games and be a nonaggressive person. This could be due to several factors such as personality, home environment, peers, and culture. Another person could play very few hours of violent video games but be more aggressive, possibly due to risk factors, than the typical player.

Aha!

Clearly there was a general trend portrayed by the line of best fit through the data points. Increased aggression could be both the cause and the result of hours spent playing violent video games. Looks of surprise and understanding showed on various faces in the class. Seeing both the relationship and the variability at the same time allowed us to discuss this topic and give equal importance to both causal relationships and uncertain outcomes. It eliminated an overly simplistic deliberation that focused on either cause-effect relationships or individual variability.

Success

What an incredible feeling of success! Finally, I had determined how I could convey information so it could not be as easily discounted. We then continued with video clips, worksheets and discussion and made some small progress in approaching a complex and controversial point with open minds—my primary goal. As a caveat, I emphasize that this approach did not convince everyone in the class. However, in general, more open dialogue and intellectual curiosity materialized with this approach.

Sex Differences

Using graphic statistical information has also helped students understand another topic that is often perplexing. We discuss sex differences between men and women, which is a topic that is often simplified and divisive. Some students in the class are unwilling to concede there are any sex differences, saying, "There are no differences in men and women; they are equal. Women can do anything men can do and vice versa."

It sounds very egalitarian, fair, and open minded. Importantly, there are other people in the class who argue that there are noteworthy differences in various measures—physical strength, spatial ability, number of words spoken in a day, and emotional expression. They will just as emphatically assert that men and women are very different. These two groups can argue unproductively without making any progress in improving the level of truth, understanding, or tolerance. Some current events such as women serving in military combat roles make this topic very contentious.

Effect Size

Discussing effect size has been the most convincing approach for this topic. By superimposing normal distribution curves and demonstrating the difference in means, students can visually compare group differences in relation to the total range.

For the majority of variables, the effect size is small (Hyde, 2007). It is difficult to draw two normal distributions separated by a mere 20 percent of one standard deviation. A few dependent measures have moderate or large effect sizes, sometimes as much as one or two standard deviations. However, even then, the total range is much greater than the difference between the means. Knowing a person's sex does not determine their individual measure on a variable.

For example, some women throw a softball faster than some men even though this measure has a discernible difference between the two group means with most men throwing faster than the average woman.

When students can see the difference in means and the overlap between the two groups, they can balance the two conflicting forces—group differences and individual variation. Quantifying effect size for various measures helps students reduce the uncertainty inherent in a discussion of sex differences.

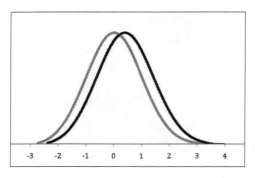

Figure 2. A normal distribution used to convey mean and standard deviation to students. Two curves present varying degrees of overlap related to effect size.

Seeing ranges, standard deviations, and differences in means graphically is helpful in counteracting stereotypes and discrimination. Group differences do exist, but they do not define the individuals within those groups. Sometimes differences are so small that they are interesting and statistically significant; however, they are not particularly meaningful considering individual variation. Surprisingly, it is counterproductive to discount differences when they do exist. Students use extreme cases to bolster preconceived notions about sex differences.

Lessons Learned

Many instructors use statistics to communicate complex ideas to their students. Mathematical and graphical representations are very powerful and insightful. Quantitative and spatial information accurately explain complex relationships. A dread of math fails to appear when students see graphs presented casually and in simple terms. They understand and articulate the critical relationships in complicated topics better than those ideas sold by oversimplification in popularized discussions and theories.

Being a wise information-processer entails managing ambiguity and balancing conflicting forces. Teaching methods that reduce cognitive ambiguity with data and weigh competing considerations can assist students to develop their thinking skills. In contrast, ideas presented in black-and-white (either/or) terms stifle accurate assessment. Helping students see the multitude of variables in context and perspective helps instructors overcome the strongly held prior convictions of learners.

Dig Down

Learning and growth involve change that can be difficult and painful. This is as true for the instructor as it is for the student. The lesson is clear, when teaching a critical concept becomes difficult, dig down and enroll alternative tactics. Teachers continually need to feed their divergent (creative) thinking skills when planning teaching strategy. Effective teaching often requires accepting humility as a springboard to betterment.

Success in teaching affords us satisfaction in two ways. First, we receive vicarious joy when students enjoy their learning. Second, even when students are uncomfortable with academic challenges we can celebrate success when we promote new skills and learning.

References

Anderson, C. A., and Bushman, B. J. (2001). Effects of Violent Video Games on Aggressive Behavior, Aggressive Cognition, Aggressive Affect, Physiological Arousal, and Prosocial Behavior: A Meta-Analytic Review of the Scientific Literature. Psychological Science (Wiley-Blackwell), 12(5), 353.

Hyde, J. (2007). New Directions in the Study of Gender Similarities and Differences. Current Directions In Psychological Science (Wiley-Blackwell), 16(5), 259-263. doi:10.1111/j.1467-8721.2007.00516.x

Savion, L. (2009). Clinging to Discredited Beliefs: The Larger Cognitive Story. Journal of The Scholarship of Teaching And Learning, 9(1), 81-92.

17

A Clear Reward

BLAZING A NEW PATH

Billy Sammons, PhD, also known as Dr. B

> *[I]nnovation comes from people meeting up in the hallways or calling each other at 10:30 at night with a new idea, or because they realized something that shoots holes in how we've been thinking about a problem.*
>
> ~Steve Jobs

I have taught a variety of college courses online and traditionally for more than 25 years. As a graduate student in 1985, I developed a computerized practice test program for undergraduates enrolled in the Introduction to Psychology course at Washington State University. This program led to a thesis and MS in psychology, along with several published papers in professional journals.

My doctoral research in experimental cognitive psychology investigated individual differences in the role of working memory on text comprehension. The surprising results of these published studies prompted considerable international research by other investigators in efforts to replicate the findings. As a result, converging evidence for new theories about the role of working memory on learning continues to mount.

My story of clarity developed over time. It took many years of observing student online behavior before I finally could construct a self-paced course to address the main obstacles to student success. As a testament to its effectiveness, I have witnessed a high level of motivation in the beginning of each online session. In their personal biographies, filled with past discretion and newfound hopes for the future, I found a common theme. Almost every student claims to understand the importance of higher education to complete their goals.

It Is All about Time

What happens after the first few weeks of an online course? Reality surfaces revealing what it takes to meet success in this learning environment. It quickly sinks in that a lack of time management skills creates a crafty roadblock. Time management skills play an especially important role in completing online courses. Inefficient use of time out shadows the will to persevere. Seeing this happen time and time again, I needed to find a way to help students maintain their enthusiasm.

A Change in Student Interactions Is the Key

The internet has exacerbated the fact that people are predominately visual beings. Students are much more likely to watch a video than read. Since I could not confirm that students were reading my detailed feedback, I wondered what I could do to facilitate interaction.

Better seeing the need to emulate the face-to-face environment, I began searching for software tools that could promote friendlier student-instructor interchanges. I looked at video screen capture programs and learned how they work. Some worked easier than others, and there was quite a steep learning curve.

Teaching online takes a tremendous amount of effort, and at times, it seems nearly impossible to get students to comply with basic expectations. Technology affords teachers the opportunity to implement nifty programs designed to enhance the process. However, as many of us know, the burden to embrace these innovative programs lies on the shoulders of the students.

Since there is a strong tendency for online students to be underprepared as self-directed learners, I created a short course to address the many foundational learning skills, encourage participation, and be, at least, somewhat entertaining.

Address Critical Skills and Boost Success

Online courses can be intimidating because many new online learners are unsure how to perform. The purpose of self-paced training is to help all online students successfully complete any program by covering a series of critical factors related to online learning.

I designed modules to address each factor. Many initially enthusiastic students who are not familiar with the ins and outs of self-directed learning have a difficult time maintaining their momentum.

My program contains strategies for success that I have shared, and continue to share, with my students. Some new learners become confused about online learning and believe it offers the opportunity to get a high grade without having to do much work. While online learning is more convenient, it is not necessarily easier. In fact, recent research has shown that online learning can be more difficult than taking a traditional course. How could that be?

Motivation Is the Key Factor to Address

The challenge of online learning points directly to the self-motivation factor. In a traditional course, there is a teacher at the front of the room and usually the students all focus on the same tasks. The task is to listen to the lectures from the teacher, take down notes about the homework assignments, and participate in the learning process.

In this social environment, students often see one another in the parking lot when arriving, join the same clubs, participate in sports together, play in the band, and/or engage in a variety of extracurricular activities. Education in this scenario is an active person-to-person experience.

Overcoming Isolation

However, online courses isolate students. Most learn alone with very limited, to no, face-to-face communication. Of course, hybrid courses meet in a classroom a few times during the term, while the majority of online courses function exclusively in the virtual environment. Yes, a growing trend exists to enable video technology for conferencing and collaborating, but this is much different from meeting in a study hall, at the local café, or pizza parlor.

In other words, when students engage in online learning, they typically do so from their home, office, or somewhere that is conducive to taking a course without distractions. Having an email buddy classmate helps build some form of relationship, but true social interaction remains severely limited. Online learning presents great motivational challenges, especially for students accustomed to attending conventional school.

The Motivated Must Get Involved

Creating a self-paced orientation taught me "if you build it, they will come" does not apply to education. Presented with an opportunity to engage in a success program, many students choose to do less rather than more. How did I get them involved?

I have reservations about offering extra credit. A tendency exists to avoid completing expected tasks, especially if students realize extra credit comes easier. Nonetheless, in order to foster participation, I decided to offer extra credit during those first two weeks when the motivation to succeed is at its highest. In fact, I even send out the link to the program as soon as registrar enters the students—about a week before the session begins.

The orientation consists of five quizzes and students must average 70 percent in order to complete the training successfully. I developed the questions from those materials. Therefore, learners cannot pass the course unless they watch the videos and read the short lectures.

Amazingly, offering the training as extra credit tripled participation. Successful completion rates doubled, and I began offering partial credit for students who averaged 60 percent or higher. I learned that students will participate and stay with it when there is some clear reward for their effort.

What is the bottom line? There are many ways to teach for success online; it just takes instructor-determination to find the path that surmounts the many obstacles.

About the Contributors

Ricardo Anderson, PhD

Dr. Anderson has more than 15 years of professional experience in higher education and as a school administrator from the Midwest of the United States. Currently, Dr. Ricardo Anderson serves as an adjunct instructor in leadership for the master's and doctoral programs at the International Business School of Scandinavia and is a grant writer for profit and not-for-profit organizations. Dr. Anderson is actively working on three publications entitled, "Reflections of a Servant Leader," "The Realness of Workplace Bullying in Corporate America," and "The Underrepresented: The Homeless." Dr. Anderson enjoys collaborating with colleagues from all disciplines and is a life-long learner.

Dr. Anderson received his bachelor's degree in broad field science, history and education from Marquette University and earned his first master's degree from

Springfield College in organizational management and human services. His second master's degree is in educational leadership and was conferred with his PhD in Leadership and Learning from Cardinal Stritch University. Dr. Anderson relaxes and finds comfort in spending time with his wife, Marisa, and their six children.

Zenobia Bailey

Zenobia brings a wealth of experience to the education arena, having taught K-College. Currently, she is an adjunct assistant professor for the University of Maryland University College where she teaches online courses:
- Principles and Strategies of Successful Learning Mass Media Studies
- Communication and Public Relations Seminars
- Case Studies in Ethics
- Case Studies in Leadership

Working many years as a staff and consultant in the general field of communications, her experience runs the gamut, including:
- Hospital public relations
- Researcher for the National Association of Community Health Centers
- Consultant to the Lower Bucks County Chamber of Commerce
- Minority Enterprise Small Business Investment Companies
- Reflection House (a bed and breakfast) and a number of other organizations

Her personal passions include advocacy for families, particularly women and children, social media consulting to The One World Center for Autism, and writing health and wellness articles. Asked about her current course, Bailey replied, "It's a course that empowers students with a cadre of tools for success! The tools include learning strategies and time management. I've thoroughly enjoyed teaching the hybrid course in a traditional format on the Adelphi campus and now online from the beautiful state of Washington."

Erik Bean, EdD
Dr. Bean is a dynamic public speaker helping teachers improve instruction and employ social networks to engage students. He publishes books and a number of digital downloads through Brigantine Media's Compass Educational Division.

He has taught for many years at American Public University, Art Institute of Michigan, Davenport University, University of Phoenix, Wayne State University, and Wayne County Community College and is a member of the Association for the Advancement of Computers in Education (AACE), the National Council of Teachers of English (NCTE), and serves as Board Member for The Customer Experience Institute.

Dave Bequette
I taught secondary school for 32 years in the Orland Unified School District and completed my 35th year as an adjunct faculty member with Butte College this year. I

served on WASC school accreditation committees at the secondary level and taught in the areas of business subjects and technology. My current college classes include Introduction to Computing and Microsoft Office courses. I am a certified online instructor. I served as a speaker for many educational organizations during my career and have written several articles for *Teaching for Success*. I live in Chico, California.

Gary D. Brown, MA
  Educational background:
  - BS in Business Administration at Northwestern State University (NSU)
  - MA in Adult Education at NSU
  - Masters +30 at NSU

  Teaching certifications:
  - Special Education Mild/Moderate
  - Adult Education Instruction
  - Educational Diagnostician

  Current employment
  - Adjunct Instructor at Louisiana State University Alexandria
  - Adjunct Instructor at Bossier Parish Community College, Northwestern State University
  - Educational Diagnostician for Rapides Parish School Board

  Previous employment
  - Mortgage banker from 1995 to 2004
  - Special education teacher for the Natchitoches Parish School Board

Laura Roach Eyler, MA Applied Linguistics

Laura, raised in a small town in Central Illinois, learned the wanderlust from her dad, who always said there was more to life than one's hometown. She is currently an associate faculty teaching ELP and ESL at Cascadia Community College.

Annie Abbott Foerster

Annie is a dynamic and energetic teacher whose passions for learning and teaching radiate as enthusiasm of her students. She finds creative ways to inspire students to care about the topic at hand and eagerly participate in discovery. Annie often leads her students to knowledge through 'Dialogue Learning' and in-class-workshop formats. She has interacted with learners in many adult education environments including college classrooms, prisons, corporate training, and volunteer leadership settings. Her lively and compelling curricula have been very effective in inspiring people to implement their learning in practical, everyday ways and in instigating the change they wish to see.

As an adjunct faculty for New Hope Christian College in Honolulu, Hawai`i, she is also enrolled at Fuller Seminary in the Master of Arts in Global Leadership degree program. She previously earned an MA in Religion. Annie is a regional pastor in her church, and she loves connecting with people in the community. Annie enjoys hanging out a home with her husband and several cats; her interests include traveling, reading, cooking, hiking, volunteer activities, and creative arts. Her daughter, an elementary school teacher, and her son-in-law, a police officer, live in California. A couple of little-known facts are that Annie has founded two successful restaurants and has driven race cars competitively.

Stacey Frazier

Stacey is a faculty member at Northern Oklahoma College. Throughout her life, she always wanted to become a teacher. Stacey earned her undergraduate degree in English at Oklahoma State University with an emphasis in secondary education. Her ultimate goal was to teach high school Language Arts; however, after only one semester, she began her family and priorities changed.

While raising her son, she worked at Oklahoma State University (OSU) as the assistant to a department chair. During this time, she encountered college students on a daily basis, counseling and advising them. She also worked on funding issues and course scheduling for the department. While working at OSU, Stacey chose to pursue a Master of Business Administration degree. After earning her MBA, Stacey taught a composition course at a local community college. Walking into that classroom relit the fire Stacey once had for teaching. It was at that point when she realized that her true calling in life was to teach. After completing that class, Stacey chose to leave her post at OSU, become an adjunct faculty member at the community college, and begin a doctoral program focusing on curriculum and teaching in education.

After three years of teaching as an adjunct instructor, she accepted a tenure-track position. Stacey strives to be the teacher whom the students can come to for academic instruction and life lessons. Being a part of someone's life and helping that person impact society is an amazing feeling and something Stacey cherishes whenever she teaches.

Melissa Alvarez Mangual
Melissa is an adjunct faculty and the Research Coordinator in the Office of Institutional Effectiveness at Eastern Florida State College, (formerly Brevard Community College). She teaches Introduction to International Studies both online and in a traditional classroom.

Melissa has a bachelor's degree from Florida State University, master's degree from DePaul University, and is working on a doctorate (EdD) at Northeastern University.

With 13 years of work experience in higher education and organizational development, she:
- Co-established the Chicago branch of the Posse Foundation, Inc.
- Worked in Educational Equity at the Pennsylvania State University
- Served at the international headquarters for Habitat for Humanity

Melissa is married, raising a young daughter, and living with two rescue dogs. She serves on the Board of Directors for Big Brothers Big Sisters of Central Florida.

Jana McCurdy

Jana originally attended the University of Idaho with the intention of majoring in math so she could teach high school. However, she loved her introductory psychology class so much she rewarded herself for doing her math problems by reading her psychology textbook. She later became fascinated by a class in Engineering Psychology.

Human factors combined a love of math and analysis with a desire to help people. Her master's thesis involved vending machine warning labels (risk perception). She has since seen those warning labels everywhere she has travelled: Australia, Tokyo, Singapore, New Guinea, Mexico, Canada, and all parts of the U.S. She also did an internship at General Motors in Detroit studying navigational displays and collision avoidance alarms.

Then, she went to Virginia Tech and worked a couple years in the Vehicle Simulation Lab and the Management Systems Lab.

After teaching overseas, and doing public outreach for the state of Idaho, Jana moved with her family to Boise in 2007 and started teaching college classes. She currently enjoys teaching at the College of Western Idaho. She and her husband have two grown children. Their family enjoys hiking, camping, playing pinochle, reading, and watching football games and movies.

Stephanie A. Melick, MA

Stephanie is an adjunct instructor and program advisor at Centenary College, NJ, with the School of Professional Studies. This is an accelerated program for adults seeking their associate's, bachelor's, and/or master's degree.

Stephanie also teaches traditional students at Caldwell (soon to be) University, NJ. She received her undergraduate degree in education from Felician College and a master's in psychology from Montclair State University. Prior to initiating a second career in higher education, Stephanie was a teacher, counselor, and administrator in New Jersey public schools for more than 30 years and a mental health worker for five years.

She is a trained psychological first-aid responder (TLC), a Literacy Volunteer, serves on the advisory board for Morris County Violence Prevention Coalition, and recently completed the Child Advocate certificate program through Montclair State University.

Martha Parrott, EdD

Dr. Parrott is Associate Professor of Mathematics at Northeastern State University. She is a former classroom teacher whom today prepares future educators. Dr. Parrott also chairs the MEd Mathematics Education program and supports the continuing professional development of practicing K-12 mathematics teachers. Her role with the university includes serving as the NSU Director of the Oklahoma Elementary Mathematics Specialist program and Director of the NSU Mathematics Clinic, a service learning experience that connects students to the community.

Recognized nationally for her effective mathematics teaching, Dr. Parrott is the recipient of many honors and awards. She is a DaVinci Fellow, a prestigious award that recognizes higher education faculty known for creative approaches to teaching and learning. In the classroom, Dr. Parrott strives to impact the teaching efficacy beliefs of her own students. Therefore, as they enter the profession they will be better prepared for the realities of the classroom and the teachable moments that await them. Her students comment how she positively transformed their beliefs about learning and teaching mathematics. They believe they are genuinely better people for having been in her classes.

Pamela Porter, PhD

Dr. Porter is an adjunct instructor of psychology at Ashland Technical and Community College. She received her PhD in Educational Psychology at Capella University submitting a dissertation, *Teachers' Perception of Bullying in Kentucky, grades K-12*. She also wrote and presented a summary of her work on the topic of bullying.

For the past three years, she received the Teaching and Learning Excellence award from Ashland Technical and Community College. In addition, she volunteers as a reviewer for the APA in the Society for Teaching Psychology Division. She contributes to her local community working on many academic and literacy endeavors. In addition to teaching and volunteering, Dr. Porter works as a freelance writer. She is currently launching two websites, www.raisingtodayschildren.com and www.educatingtodayschildren.com.

She can also be found at www.phdraisinggirls.com for a lighter look at raising teenage girls and dealing with mid-life issues. She currently resides in Eastern Kentucky with her husband, Dwain, and three teenage daughters. Dr. Porter can be contacted at Pamela.phd3@gmail.com.

Billy Sammons, PhD

I earned my PhD in Experimental Psychology at Washington State University, Pullman, WA, campus. Learning and memory as it applies to reading comprehension is my specialty. I have been teaching online for more than 15 years and enjoy the flexibility of the virtual learning environment. My research focuses on working memory and the effects on reading comprehension.

I also spent ten years teaching traditional classes at California State University, Sacramento. It was there that I started a mentoring program for lower-achieving high school students. We paired college students with high school students, and the program gained enough success to expand to all 23 campuses.

I recently moved from Oregon to Iowa to help my life partner take care of her aging parents who refuse to move off the farm. For fun, I raise Rhode Island Red chickens, exercise regularly, and play piano. Listen to my music at OrganicPiano.com.

Also, visit YouTube, www.youtube.com/watch?v=LEAycI38tJQ to see a video summary of a documentary aired on *PBS* about my experiences working with a community in Oregon on a common project.

Brian Shmaefsky, PhD

Brian is a professor of biology and service learning coordinator at Lone Star College-Kingwood (formerly Kingwood College). His teaching duties include instructing and coordinating the curriculum for non-majors biology. He earned a Bachelor of Science in Biology from Brooklyn College, an Master of Science in Biology (Environmental Physiology) from Southern Illinois University, an EdD in Science Education from Southern Illinois University, and completed PhD studies in Environmental Physiology at the University of Illinois.

His publications include many peer reviewed articles on science education. He authored several books on biotechnology, human anatomy and physiology, science pedagogy, and medical advances.

Dr. Shmaefsky also worked as a production biochemist for industry. He continues to consult with biotechnology industries. His current passions include environmental advocacy efforts particularly related to environmental endocrine disrupters. Brian currently volunteers on many regional, national, and international environmental policy and public education committees.

Ruth E. Starr, PhD

Dr. Starr lives in Virginia and works full time for the U.S. Federal Government in Washington, DC. She received her Bachelor of Science Degree through Upper Iowa University's Distance Learning Program and her Master of Science Degree in Distance Education through Capella

University School of Education. She completed her PhD research in the School of Education at Capella University. Dr. Starr continues to study the role of service learning and community service in preparing graduates for the transition to a career. She is a tutor and mentor to high school seniors and college freshman.

Richard Sumpter, MPA

In 1963, I concluded eight years of seminary training—four years majoring in philosophy and four more studying theology and scripture—and was then ordained a Catholic priest. I spent the next five years working in parishes and taught in parochial high schools. In 1968, I left active ministry and joined the War on Poverty.

As an employee of the U.S. Office of Economic Opportunity, I worked with community action agencies in Kansas, Nebraska, Iowa, and Missouri. I trained boards and staff in strategic planning and community development. During these years, I returned to night school and in 1976 earned a Bachelor of Arts in Public Administration.

In 1979, I went to Harvard to attend the Kennedy School of Government, and received my MPA in 1980. In 1981, the War on Poverty ended with an unconditional surrender and the federal agency was abolished. In 1983, I went to work for the Federal Emergency Management Agency doing off-site safety planning for nuclear power plants. I also began teaching strategic planning as an adjunct instructor at two universities in the Kansas City metro area.

In 1990, I transferred to the U.S. Environmental Protection Agency where I am currently employed as the Regional Planning Coordinator.

In 1989, I began teaching at the Baker University School of Professional and Graduate Studies. This was an accelerated adult program. I subsequently taught more than 270 courses in various disciplines ranging from the business program to the Master of Liberal Arts. I was named Instructor of the Year in 2008.

I have developed and taught more than a dozen courses in ethics, philosophy, theology, and mythology. I have also served on numerous faculty committees dealing with curriculum development and accreditation. I just completed work on the development of a new degree program, Master of Arts in Organizational Leadership.

I plan on retiring from EPA in 2014 and devoting myself to whatever academic pursuits interest me.

Made in the USA
San Bernardino, CA
07 August 2014